A Birthday Treasury

Writings Festive and Joyful,

Wise and Inspiring

A Birthday Treasury

Selected by Douglas A. Drake

HALLMARK EDITIONS

A Birthday Treasury

 *A New Year*

Here's a clean year, a white year.
Reach your hand and take it.
You are the builder,
And no one else can make it.

See what it is that waits here,
Whole and new;
It's not a year only,
But a world for you!

MARY CAROLYN DAVIES

Choice and Compromise

We are the sum total of all the choices we have made.
There is scarcely an hour of the day in which we are
not called upon to make choices of one sort or another, trivial or far-reaching. We are all beset by
choices. What time shall I get up or go to bed? What
shall I wear? What shall I eat? Whom shall I see?
Will I take the road to the left or the one to the right?

Then come the somewhat bigger choices: What
shall I do with my life? How much am I willing to
give of myself, of my time, of my love? What kind
of career shall I decide on—and why? That is, do I
want fame, money, personal satisfaction, self-ex-
pression, or some other value?

Just as all living is adjustment and readjustment,
so all choice, to some extent, must be compromise
between reality and a dream of perfection. We must
try to bring the reality as close to that dream of perfection as we can, but we must not demand of it the
impossible. It is only an approximation that anyone
can reach, but the closer one tries to approximate it,
the more he will grow. If he keeps his dream of perfection and strains toward it, he will come closer to
achieving it than if he rejects the reality because it
was not perfection.

ELEANOR ROOSEVELT

Is Life Worth Living?

The question, "Is life worth living?" has been much discussed; particularly by those who think it is not, many of whom have written at great length in support of their view and by careful observance of the laws of health enjoyed for long terms of years the honors of successful controversy.

AMBROSE BIERCE

Give Us, Lord, A Bit O' Sun

Give us, Lord, a bit o' sun,
A bit o' work and a bit o' fun;
Give us in all the struggle and sputter
Our daily bread and a bit o' butter;
Give us health, our keep to make,
An' a bit to spare for others' sake;
Give us, too, a bit of song
And a tale, and a book to help us along.
Give us, Lord, a chance to be
Our goodly best, brave, wise and free,
Our goodly best for ourself, and others,
Till all men learn to live as brothers.

OLD ENGLISH PRAYER

In the very rare and treasured times when I have my solitude, my greatest reward is that I am able to make some infinitesimally small progress toward acquaintance with myself, something you cannot do unless you can be alone and therefore free.

There are other fruits of solitude. It enables me to avail myself a little bit more of the pleasures so many of us look forward to in life, like being able to read and concentrate on what we're reading, something I find very difficult to do when I'm sur-rounded by loving friends and the intrusion of well-meaning people. I find that when I am home in Nyack I read a whole page of a book, a book that I've been hungering for, and I have to go back and read it again because I virtually don't know what I've read. My mind has been shooting off in other directions—to what I must do tomorrow, to what I forgot to do today, or to having to phone somebody about some quite unimportant matter. But when I get to hide in my garden, or go on a long walk, or settle down briefly in Cuernavaca, my mind relaxes and it is receptive to the things I am so anxious to enjoy.

We live in a very tense society. We are pulled apart as if by centrifugal force and we all need to learn how to pull ourselves together. Pull ourselves together—we all use that phrase, but too many of us aren't trained for that job of literally pulling ourselves together so that we can function as full human beings. I think that at least part of the answer lies in solitude.   HELEN HAYES

Difference is in the nature of life. It is part of our moral universe. Without difference life would become lifeless.

So I reject the ideal of total conformity, compulsory or complacent; the faith that is swallowed like pills, whole and at once, with no questions asked. I believe in helping ourselves and others to see the possibilities in viewpoints other than one's own; in encouraging the free interchange of ideas; in welcoming fresh approaches to the problems of life; in urging the fullest, most vigorous use of critical self-examination. Thus we can learn to grow together, to unite in our common search for truth within a better and a happier world.

ADLAI STEVENSON

The Senses of Life

Sometimes I think that people actually have "taken leave of their senses." We can see, hear, taste, smell, and touch, and these senses are not only the primary means of self-protection but the source of greatest delight. It is through the senses that we receive our first impressions of the world, and make our first discriminations—between beauty and ugliness, bitter and sweet, scent and odor, smoothness and roughness, music and noise, and the higher the cultivation of the senses, the more refined and cultivated the person.

The senses are cultivated by use. The painter trains himself better to see, the musician to hear, the craftsman to touch, the chef to taste and smell. The expression accompanies and follows the training. But there is an artist in us all, otherwise artists would have no audiences. The extent to which we develop the artist in ourselves measures the extent to which we appreciate not only art but *life*.

DOROTHY THOMPSON

Not in Vain

If I can stop one heart from breaking,
I shall not live in vain:
If I can ease one life the aching,
Or cool one pain,
Or help one fainting robin
Unto his nest again,
I shall not live in vain.

EMILY DICKINSON

Live Each Day

Would you fashion for yourself a seemly life?
Then do not fret over what is past and gone;
In spite of all you may have left behind
Live each day as if your life had just begun.

GOETHE

The Vital Spirit

That for which man lives is not the same thing for
all individuals nor in all ages; yet it has a common
base; what he seeks and what he must have is that
which will seize and hold his attention. Regular
meals and weatherproof lodgings will not do this
long. Play in its wide sense, as the artificial induc-

tion of sensation, including all games and all arts, will, indeed, go far to keep him conscious of himself; but in the end he wearies for realities. Study or experiment, to some rare natures, is the unbroken pastime of a life.

These are enviable natures; people shut in the house by sickness often bitterly envy them; but the commoner man cannot continue to exist upon such altitudes: his feet itch for physical adventure; his blood boils for physical dangers, pleasures, and triumphs; his fancy, the looker after new things, cannot continue to look for them in books and crucibles, but must seek them on the breathing stage of life. Pinches, buffets, the glow of hope, the shock of disappointment, furious contention with obstacles: these are the true elixir for all vital spirits, these are what they seek alike in their romantic enterprises and their unromantic dissipations. When they are taken in some pinch closer than the common, they cry, "Catch me here again!" and sure enough you catch them there again—perhaps before the week is out. It is as old as *Robinson Crusoe*; as old as man. Our race has not been strained for all these ages through that sieve of dangers that we call Natural Selection, to sit down with patience in the tedium of safety; the voices of its fathers call it forth.   ROBERT LOUIS STEVENSON

13

To Every Thing There Is a Season

To every thing there is a season, and a time
to every purpose under the heaven:
A time to be born, and a time to die; a time
to plant, and a time to pluck up that which
is planted;
A time to kill, and a time to heal; a time
to break down, and a time to build up;
A time to weep, and a time to laugh; a time
to mourn, and a time to dance;
A time to cast away stones, and a time to
gather stones together; a time to embrace,
and a time to refrain from embracing;
A time to get, and a time to lose; a time
to keep, and a time to cast away;
A time to rend, and a time to sew; a time
to keep silence, and a time to speak;
A time to love, and a time to hate; a time
of war, and a time of peace.

ECCLESIASTES 3:1-8

ARIES: *March 21 to April 20*

Aries is the sign of regeneration, initiative, and energy. If you were born in this sign, you are probably eager for experience and travel, and enjoy the active life. With people you are friendly and open-minded, but your personal ambition is to convert frequent opportunities into achievements and to have them recognized in the real world. Though self-confident and self-motivating, you nonetheless find security in both external recognition and strong ties with your family and friends.

TAURUS: *April 21 to May 21*

The most outstanding accomplishments of persons born in this sign result from physical energy and persistence. You find immediate joy in working, and you express that joy by appreciating the fruits of labor—the "good things of life"—nice surroundings, good clothes, and a plentiful table. With practical responsibilities taken care of, and secure in physical comforts, you often find further enjoyment in artistic and intellectual endeavors, and share your philosophical and aesthetic opinions, as well as your home, with people who share these noble and exciting interests.

GEMINI: *May 22 to June 21*

If you were born a Gemini, you are chiefly interested in exercising your mind, and incline towards literary and scientific activities. In either field, you are concerned with logic, consistency, and definition. Your combination of "pure" intellectuality and aesthetic sensitivity allow you to be versatile and adaptable in dealing with people and situations. You are, in fact, not only vivacious and sympathetic, but affectionate, demonstrative, and genuinely thoughtful of the comfort of others.

CANCER: *June 22 to July 23*

If you were born in this sign, you characteristically grow as a person by establishing a wider circle of personal relationships and by developing an increasingly comfortable environment. Your tolerance and sympathy lead you to make new friends, but you are loyal to your old friends at the same time. At home you are devoted and affectionate, and your sensitive, intuitive character not only helps you deal more successfully with members of your family, but also leads you to develop and enliven the physical aspects of the household environment.

LEO: *July 24 to August 23*

Leonians are considered the most self-sufficient individuals of any under the twelve signs. You establish your purposes and your standards of conduct, then set out with self-assurance to fulfill your own potential. As long as you are satisfied with your achievements you are more than glad to be noticed by others for what you are. Unless you disappoint your own expectations and become moody for a time, you tend to be magnanimous and even dramatic in personal and social relations.

VIRGO: *August 24 to September 23*

The Virgo personality is humble, modest, and humanitarian. If you were born in this sign, you are a helpful, cooperative friend and cherish and serve your family in even the most minute respects. You have a variety of genuine interests and friends in your community, but, being sensitive to people, are selective when it comes to your intimate circle of friends. You are eminently practical when it comes to expressing your opinions, but in every situation or issue you take care to tailor practicality to the human elements involved.

LIBRA: *September 24 to October 23*

A person born in Libra seeks balance, justice and security in a graceful and conciliatory manner. As an idealist, you are responsive and open to suggestion and opportunity, and your resourcefulness and versatility allow you to resolve tense situations or issues. Others are attracted to you easily, and you make a delightful companion. With your close friends you are warm, supporting, and loyal, and you seek to share new experiences with them.

SCORPIO: *October 24 to November 22*

Scorpio is associated with the capacity to make and remake yourself according to your own ideas and judgment. Intensity and concentration, though you don't make a show of these traits, are frequent vehicles of your convictions. You assume responsibility when you feel it is necessary or right to do so, and in this case you are reliable and will accept the consequences of your acts. You are a skeptical realist, but once you accept a point or a cause you will generously and loyally support it.

SAGITTARIUS: *November 23 to December 21*

As a Sagittarian, you are not only affable and enthusiastic, but high-minded and goal-directed. You are naturally philosophical—even contemplative—and you are a fine planner. At the same time, you enjoy movement, sports, and the outdoors. Your range of interests gives you a resilience to temporary disappointments and enhances greatly your value as a friend. In friendships you are exciting, often inspirational, and always honest, open, and high-minded. The same is true in business and committee affairs, where you must guard against being tactlessly straightforward and impractically idealistic in your expression.

CAPRICORN: *December 22 to January 20*

If you were born in the sign of Capricorn, then you are one of the most practical and also one of the most resourceful of individuals. Orderly, quick, and efficient, you are untiring in solving problems, large or small. Though unassuming, your inner pride urges you to seek high places and the good things in life. Your common sense and adaptability, when combined with your reliability and emotional faithfulness, make you a key member of the family.

AQUARIUS: *January 21 to February 19*

The person who is born in this sign is basically humanitarian and democratic. He is enthusiastically responsive to all kinds of people, and gregarious even though he may be quiet. Loyal, generous and hospitable, the Aquarian is also eminently intellectual and philosophical (rather than emotional) in outlook. He is capable of tremendous dedication and is quick to meet the challenges in life which are the main source of his learning. Dedicated to principles, he will devote his life to maintaining and realizing ideals he has established.

PISCES: *February 20 to March 20*

If you are a Piscean, you are outstandingly resourceful and believe yourself capable of partaking in and understanding everything. Indeed, your greatest gestures are of empathy and service to others. You are extremely sensitive, and may well be musical or artistic. You are affectionate and uncomplaining in the home, unaggressive in manner, and you do well whatever you have to do, whether it is a humble task or a distinguished one. Your intuition and competence create order from the many and varied relationships of daily existence.

I Am Content

The longer I live the more my mind dwells upon
the beauty and wonder of the world....

I have loved the feel of the grass under my feet,
and the sound of the running streams by my side.
The hum of the wind in the treetops has always
been good music to me, and the face of the fields
has often comforted me more than the faces of men.

I am in love with this world.... I have tilled its
soil, I have gathered its harvests, I have waited upon its seasons, and always have I reaped what I
have sown.

I have climbed its mountains, roamed its forests,
sailed its waters, crossed its deserts, felt the sting of
its frosts, the oppressions of its heats, the drench of
its rains, the fury of its winds, and always have
beauty and joy waited upon my goings and comings.

JOHN BURROUGHS

To See A World

To see a world in a grain of sand
And a heaven in a wild flower,
Hold Infinity in the palm of your hand
And Eternity in an hour.   BLAKE

Life

Let me but live my life from year to year,
With forward face and unreluctant soul,
Not hastening to, nor turning from the goal;
Not mourning for the things that disappear
In the dim past, not holding back in fear
From what the future veils; but with a whole
And happy heart, that pays its toll
To youth and age, and travels on with cheer.
So let the way wind up the hill or down,
Through rough or smooth, the journey will be joy;
Still seeking what I sought but when a boy,
New friendship, high adventure, and a crown,
I shall grow old, but never lose life's zest,
Because the road's last turn will be the best.

HENRY VAN DYKE

I have indeed lived nominally fifty years, but deduct out of them the hours which I have lived to other people, and not to myself, and you will find me still a young fellow. For *that* is the only true Time, which a man can properly call his own, that which he has all to himself; the rest, though in some sense he may be said to live it, is other people's time, not his.   CHARLES LAMB

The Road Not Taken

Two roads diverged in a yellow wood,
And sorry I could not travel both
And be one traveler, long I stood
And looked down one as far as I could
To where it bent in the undergrowth;

Then took the other, as just as fair,
And having perhaps the better claim,
Because it was grassy and wanted wear;
Though as for that the passing there
Had worn them really about the same,

And both that morning equally lay
In leaves no step had trodden black.
Oh, I kept the first for another day!
Yet knowing how way leads on to way,
I doubted if I should ever come back.

I shall be telling this with a sigh
Somewhere ages and ages hence:
Two roads diverged in a wood, and I—
I took the one less traveled by,
And that has made all the difference.

ROBERT FROST

Blessed is he who has found his work; let him ask no other blessedness. He has a work, a life-purpose; he has found it, and will follow it! How, as a free-flowing channel, dug and torn by noble force through the sour mud-swamp of one's existence, like an ever-deepening river there, it runs and flows; — draining-off the sour festering water, gradually from the root of the remotest grass-blade; making, instead of pestilential swamp, a green fruitful meadow with its clear-flowing stream. How blessed for the meadow itself, let the stream and its value be great or small!

Labor is Life: from the inmost heart of the Worker rises his god-given Force, the sacred celestial Life-essence breathed into him by Almighty God; from his inmost heart awakens him to all nobleness, — to all knowledge, "self-knowledge" and much else, so soon as Work fitly begins. Knowledge? The knowledge that will hold good in working, cleave thou to that; for Nature herself accredits that, says Yea to that.

Properly thou hast no other knowledge but what thou has got by working: the rest is yet all a hypothesis of knowledge; a thing to be argued of in schools, a thing floating in the clouds, in endless logic-vortices, till we try it and fix it. "Doubt, of whatever kind, can be ended by Action alone."   THOMAS CARLYLE

When a person has become seasoned by experience and has reached the age of discretion, he likes a family compliment as well as ever, but he does not lose his head over it as in the old innocent days.   MARK TWAIN

Some Special Delight

It is beyond a doubt that everyone should have time for some special delight, if only five minutes each day to seek out a lovely flower or cloud or a star, or learn a verse or brighten another's dull task. What is the use of such terrible diligence as many tire themselves out with, if they always postpone their exchange of smiles with Beauty and Joy to cling to irksome duties and relations? Unless they admit these fair, fresh, and eternal presences into their lives as they can, they must needs shut themselves out of heaven, and a gray dust settles on all existence. That the sky is brighter than the earth means little unless the earth itself is appreciated and enjoyed.   HELEN KELLER

January / Carnation

Lovely flowers are smiles of God's goodness.

SAMUEL WILBERFORCE

February / Violet

The flower of sweetest smell is shy and lowly.

WILLIAM WORDSWORTH

March / Jonquil

And the spring arose on the garden fair
Like the spirit of Love felt everywhere.

PERCY BYSSHE SHELLEY

April/Sweet Pea

Here are sweet peas, on tiptoe for a flight;
With wings of gentle flush o'er delicate white,
And taper fingers catching at all things,
To bind them all about with tiny rings.

JOHN KEATS

May/Lily of the Valley

Where scattered wild the Lily of the Vale
Its balmy essence breathes.

JAMES THOMSON

June/Rose

Yon rose-buds in the morning dew,
How pure amang the leaves sae green!

ROBERT BURNS

July/Larkspur

Earth laughs in flowers.

RALPH WALDO EMERSON

August/Gladiolus

Ye pretty daughters of the earth and sun.

SIR WALTER RALEIGH

September / Aster

The aster greets us as we pass
With her faint smile.

SARAH HELEN WHITMAN

October / Calendula

Flowers are the sweetest things that God ever
made....   HENRY WARD BEECHER

November / Chrysanthemum

Fair gift of Friendship! and her ever bright and
faultless image! welcome now thou art....

ANNA PEYRE DINNIES

December / Narcissus

The "amen!" of nature is always a flower.

OLIVER WENDELL HOLMES

Look to this day!
For it is life, the very life of life ....
For yesterday is already a dream, and tomorrow
    is only a vision;
But today, well lived, makes every yesterday
A dream of happiness, and every tomorrow a
    vision of hope.

FROM THE SANSKRIT

Visions and Ideals

The dreamers are the saviors of the world. As the
visible world is sustained by the invisible, so men,
through all their trials and sins and sordid voca-
tions, are nourished by the beautiful visions of

their solitary dreamers. Humanity cannot forget its dreamers; it cannot let their ideas fade and die; it lives in them; it knows them as the realities which it shall one day see and know.

Composer, sculptor, painter, poet, prophet, sage, these are the makers of the after-world, the architects of heaven. The world is beautiful because they have lived; without them, laboring humanity would perish.

He who cherishes a beautiful vision, a lofty ideal in his heart, will one day realize it. Columbus cherished a vision of another world, and he discovered it; Copernicus fostered the vision of a multiplicity of worlds and a wider universe and he revealed it; Buddha beheld the vision of a spiritual world of stainless beauty and perfect peace, and he entered into it.

Cherish your visions; cherish your ideals; cherish the music that stirs in your heart, the beauty that forms in your mind, the loveliness that drapes your purest thoughts, for out of them will grow all delightful conditions, all heavenly environment; of these, if you but remain true to them, your world will at last be built.   JAMES ALLEN

Life Is in Ourselves

Life is everywhere life, life in ourselves, not in what is outside us. There will be people near me, and to be a man among people and remain a man forever, not to be downhearted nor to fall in whatever misfortunes may befall me—this is life; this is the task of life. I have realized this. This idea has entered into my flesh and into my blood.

When I look back at the past and think how much time has been wasted in vain, how much time was lost in delusions, in errors, in idleness, in ignorance of how to live, how I did not value time, how often I sinned against my heart and spirit—my heart bleeds. Life is a gift, life is happiness, each minute can be an age of happiness.

FYODOR DOSTOEVSKI

Definitions of Life

"Life is the diffusion of that light which, for the happiness of men, descended upon them from heaven," said Confucius six hundred years before Christ.

"Life is the peregrination and the perfection of souls, which attain to greater and ever greater happiness," said the Brahmins of the same day.

"Life is the abnegation of self, with the purpose of attaining blessed Nirvana," said Buddha, a contemporary of Confucius.

"Life is the path of peacefulness and lowliness, for the attainment of happiness," said Lao-Tse, also a contemporary of Confucius.

"Life is that which God breathed into man's nostrils, in order that he, by fulfilling his law, might receive happiness," said the Hebrew sage, Moses. . . .

"Life is love toward God and our neighbor, which gives happiness to man," said Christ.

Such are the definitions of life which, thousands of years before our day, pointing out to men real and indestructible happiness in the place of the false and impossible happiness of the individual, solve the contradictions of human life and impart to it a reasonable sense.   LEO TOLSTOY

Take the Whole of Life

How can any change connected with time and space destroy that which is not connected with it? A man fixes his eyes upon a small, insignificant bit of his life, does not wish to see all of it, and trembles lest this tiny fragment which is dear to him should be lost. This recalls the anecdote of the madman who imagined that he was made of glass, and who, when he was thrown down, said, "Smash!" and immediately died. In order that a man may have life, he must take the whole of it, and not that small scrap of it which reveals itself in time and space. To him that taketh the whole of life there shall be added, but from him that taketh a portion of it shall be taken away even that which he hath.

LEO TOLSTOY

Live Thy Life

Live thy life,
   Young and old,
Like yon oak,
Bright in spring,
   Living gold.

TENNYSON

Birthday Thoughts

Nothing is more highly to be prized than the value of each day.   GOETHE

Man is not the creature of circumstances. Circumstances are the creatures of men.

BENJAMIN DISRAELI

A long life may not be good enough, but a good life is long enough.   BENJAMIN FRANKLIN

A wise man never puts away childish things.

SIDNEY DARK

We do not count a man's years until he has nothing else to count.   RALPH WALDO EMERSON

At twenty years of age the will reigns; at thirty the wit; at forty the judgment.

BENJAMIN FRANKLIN

The young man who has not wept is a savage, and the old man who will not laugh is a fool.

GEORGE SANTAYANA

The world is a fine place and worth fighting for.

ERNEST HEMINGWAY

Life is not long, and too much of it must not pass in idle deliberation how it shall be spent.

SAMUEL JOHNSON

The life in us is like the water in the river. It may rise this year higher than man has ever known it, and flood the parched uplands; even this may be the eventful year....

HENRY DAVID THOREAU

Sing we for love and idleness,
Naught else is worth the having.

EZRA POUND

Patience makes women beautiful in middle age.

ELLIOT PAUL

Winter is on my head, but eternal spring is in my heart. I breathe at this hour the fragrance of the lilacs, the violets and the roses, as at twenty years.

VICTOR HUGO

I'm sorry you are wiser,
I'm sorry you are taller;
I like you better foolish,
And I liked you better smaller.

ALINE KILMER

What is past is prologue.

WILLIAM SHAKESPEARE

For every thing you have missed, you have gained something else; and for every thing you gain, you lose something.   RALPH WALDO EMERSON

It is a great consolation to reflect that, among all the bewildering changes to which the world is subject, the character of woman cannot be altered.

COVENTRY PATMORE

The mind needs room to turn around in, and when the future doesn't provide this dimension, one chooses of necessity whatever spaciousness the remembered past affords.   JESSAMYN WEST

Work in Faith

No ray of sunlight is ever lost, but the green which it awakes into existence needs time to sprout, and it is not always granted to the sower to see the harvest. All work that is worth anything is done in faith.

ALBERT SCHWEITZER

Birthday Candles

Have you ever thought that the candles on a birthday cake can represent accomplishments as well as years? The little things we've done to help others—perhaps a thoughtful prayer, an encouraging word or a helping hand when it was needed.

Age should not be counted merely by the number of years we live, but also by the good we accomplish during these years. Each candle on our birthday cake, therefore, can be a symbol of what we have done to enrich the lives of others as well as our own.

JAMES KELLER

Every Moment Is Now

In nature every moment is now; the past is always swallowed and forgotten; the coming only is sacred. Nothing is secure but life, transition, the energizing spirit. No love can be bound by oath or covenant to secure it against a higher love. No truth so sublime but it may be trivial tomorrow in the light of new thoughts. People wish to be settled; only as far as they are unsettled is there any hope for them.

Life is a series of surprises. We do not guess today the mood, the pleasure, the power of tomorrow, when we are building up our being. Of lower states, of acts of routine and sense, we can tell somewhat; but the masterpieces of God, the total growths and universal movements of the soul...are incalculable. I can know that truth is divine and helpful; but how it shall help me I can have no guess, for *so to be* is the sole inlet of *so to know*. The new position of the advancing man has all the powers of the old, yet has them all new. It carries in its bosom all the energies of the past, yet is itself an exhalation of the morning. I cast away in this new moment all my once hoarded knowledge, as vacant and vain. Now for the first time seem I to know anything rightly. The simplest words—we do not know what they mean except when we love and aspire.

RALPH WALDO EMERSON

Life Is Opportunity

On his seventieth birthday, Henry Wadsworth Long-fellow described his feelings in a letter to a younger friend:

You do not know yet what it is to be 70 years old. I will tell you, so that you may not be taken by surprise when your turn comes. It is like climbing the Alps. You reach a snow-crowned summit, and see behind you the deep valley stretching miles and miles away, and before you other summits higher and whiter which you may have strength to climb or may not. Then you sit down and meditate, and wonder which it will be. That is the whole story, amplify it as you may. All that one can say is, that life is opportunity.

Youth

Youth is not a time of life—it is a state of mind. It is not a matter of ripe cheeks, red lips, and supple knees; it is a temper of the will, a quality of the imagination, a vigor of the emotions; it is a freshness of the deep spring of life.

Youth means a temperamental predominance of courage over timidity, of the appetite of adventure over love of ease. This often exists in a man of fifty more than in a boy of twenty.

Nobody grows old by merely living a number of years; people grow old only by deserting their ideals. Years wrinkle the skin, but to give up enthusiasm wrinkles the soul. Worry, doubt, self-distrust, fear, and despair—these are the long, long years that bow the head and turn the growing spirit back to the dust.

Whether seventy or sixteen, there is in every being's heart the love of wonder, the sweet amazement at the stars and the starlike things and thoughts, the undaunted challenge of events, the unfailing childlike appetite for what next, and the joy and the game of life.

You are as young as your faith, as old as your doubt; as young as your self-confidence, as old as your fear; as young as your hope, as old as your despair.   SAMUEL ULLMAN

Grow Old Along With Me

Grow old along with me!
The best is yet to be,
The last of life, for which the first was made:
Our times are in His hand
Who saith "A whole I planned,
Youth shows but half; trust God: see all nor
        be afraid!"

ROBERT BROWNING

44

January / Garnet

The garnet is a stone having a wide range of colors, but distinguished by its bluish tint. First used as a gem by the Egyptians, it was regarded as a protection against accidents during travel and later as a symbol of long and lasting friendship. Today it is still given as a sign of loyalty, love, and good cheer.

February / Amethyst

The amethyst, a deep purple gem, in ancient times was thought to keep its wearer from becoming intoxicated with strong drink. It was used as jewelry by the Egyptians and is still used for episcopal rings. Today it is generally regarded as a symbol of peace, satisfaction, and good fortune.

March/Aquamarine

The aquamarine is a stone of transparent sea-green or delicate bluish-green color. Once thought to endow its wearer with amiability and a quick wit, it today is a symbol of good luck and pleasure.

April/Diamond

The hardest substance known to man, this brilliant stone derives its name from a Greek word meaning "invincible." The two largest brilliants known (now among the Crown Jewels of England) were cut from the famous Cullinan gem, which in its raw state weighed 3106 carats, or 1⅓ pounds. Today the diamond signifies joy and security.

May/Emerald

The emerald is a deep green precious stone which was known to Egyptians as early as 1650 B.C. The ancients believed that it helped women in childbirth and drove off evil spirits that caused many common afflictions. It later became a symbol of eloquence and strong memory, and was believed to guarantee its wearer a happy and successful life.

June/Pearl

As technically defined by its manner of formation, the pearl is quite common and varied in its specific origin. The iridescent pearl from oysters, however, is a beautiful and highly prized jewel. Symbolizing health, integrity, and good fortune, it is given as a token of the highest friendship.

July/Ruby

This deep red precious gem was long ago thought to preserve health and also to have the power to reconcile disputes. In modern times it has become perhaps the most prized of jewels, and it symbolizes fulfillment and power.

August/Peridot

A deep yellowish-green stone, the peridot in ancient times was thought to protect its wearer against harm, and was also worn as a charm to magically increase the physical beauty of both men and women. Today, more generally than then, it stands for contentment, joy and pleasure.

September/Sapphire

The sapphire is a transparent precious gem ranging in color from pale blue to deep indigo. It was once worn as a symbol of wisdom and high thoughts, and has become almost as highly valued a jewel as the diamond. The sapphire stands for prosperity, happiness, and faithfulness.

October / Opal

The opal is a precious translucent stone of many colors, often mixed and glittering together with a wonderful brilliance. (The purely black and purely colorless stones are very rare.) According to ancient legend, the opal was thought to be beneficial to the eyesight. It is worn today in rings and necklaces, and is a sign of affection and wisdom.

November / Topaz

The topaz is a transparent semiprecious stone, usually pink or honey yellow in color. It was once thought to protect its wearer against danger, and was also considered a symbol of generosity—perhaps because of its frequently large size (one crystal weighing 600 lbs. has been found in Brazil). Today it symbolizes joy of living, gladness, and delight.

December / Turquoise

The turquoise, ranging in color from sky-blue to green, was long ago used in Persia and Mexico as an ornamental stone for tools, weapons, clothing, and mosaic art. Ancients wore the stone as a protection against falls. It has since become symbolic of gaiety and laughter.

What Is Time?

What is time? The shadow on the dial, the striking
of the clock, the running of the sand day and night,
summer and winter, months, years, centuries—these
are but arbitrary and outward signs, the measure of
Time, not Time itself. Time is the life of the soul.

HENRY WADSWORTH LONGFELLOW

The Highest Art

I know of no more encouraging fact than the un-
questionable ability of man to elevate his life by a
conscious endeavor. It is something to be able to
paint a particular picture, or to carve a statue, and
so to make a few objects beautiful; but it is far
more glorious to carve and paint the very atmos-
phere and medium through which we look, which
morally we can do.

To affect the quality of the day, that is the highest of arts. Every man is tasked to make his life,
even in its details, worthy of the contemplation of
his most elevated and critical hour.

HENRY DAVID THOREAU

The Power of Imagination

How infinitely superior to our physical senses are
those of the mind! The spiritual eye sees not only
rivers of water but of air. It sees the crystals of the
rock in rapid sympathetic motion, giving enthusiastic obedience to the sun's rays, then sinking back
to rest in the night. The whole world is in motion
to the center.

So also sounds. We hear only woodpeckers and

squirrels and the rush of turbulent streams. But imagination gives us the sweet music of tiniest insect wings, enables us to hear, all around the world, the vibration of every needle, the waving of every bole and branch, the sound of stars in circulation like particles in the blood. The Sierra canyons are full of avalanche debris—we hear them boom again, and we read the past sounds from present conditions. Again we hear the earthquake rock-falls.

Imagination is usually regarded as a synonym for the unreal. Yet is true imagination healthful and real, no more likely to mislead than the coarse senses. Indeed, the power of imagination makes us infinite.

JOHN MUIR

Untold Novelties

To every one of us the world was once as fresh and new as to Adam. And then, long before we were susceptible of any other mode of instruction, Nature took us in hand, and every minute of waking life brought its educational influence, shaping our actions into rough accordance with Nature's laws, so that we might not be ended untimely by too gross disobedience. Nor should I speak of this process of education as past for anyone, be he as old as he may.

For every man the world is as fresh as it was at the first day, and as full of untold novelties for him who has the eyes to see them.

THOMAS HENRY HUXLEY

I Meant To Do my Work Today

I meant to do my work today—
But a brown bird sang in the apple tree,
And a butterfly flitted across the field,
And all the leaves were calling me.

And the wind went sighing over the land
Tossing the grasses to and fro,
And a rainbow held out its shining hand—
So what could I do but laugh and go?

RICHARD LE GALLIENNE

Moderation

To do anything in life, large and small, in every department of it, I believe we were meant to take a reasonable length of time, and not to exhibit either unreasonable haste or unreasonable sloth. It took me so long to learn this. In fact, I haven't learned it entirely. I often find myself tearing through my mail or leaving a scant few minutes between this task and the next; going, sometimes literally, and sometimes figuratively, on the double. But sooner or later I remind myself to slow down, and the job gets itself done just the same.   FAITH BALDWIN

The Aim of Life

We live in deeds, not years;
    in thoughts, not breaths;
In feelings, not in figures on a dial.
We should count time by heart-throbs.
    He most lives
Who thinks most, feels the noblest,
    acts the best.
And he whose heart beats quickest
    lives the longest.

PHILIP JAMES BAILEY

Some Small Delight

Give me this day some small delight,
Some simple joy to cheer my soul,
A singing bird upon the bough,
A drifting cloud in sky's blue bowl;
The pealing laughter of my child,
The glint of sunlight on his hair,
The feel of his warm hand in mine,
Of these dear things make me aware;
A blossom in the garden spot,
The music of the poplar trees,
The fragrance of a dew-washed earth,
What could enchant me more than these?
Grant me perception that I may
Live deeply through this chartless day,
And when I go to sleep tonight
Be thankful for each small delight.

MILLY WALTON

To Live Fully

To be concentrated means to live fully in the present, in the here and now, and not to think of the next thing to be done, while I am doing something right now. Needless to say that concentration must be practiced most of all by people who love each other. They must learn to be close to each other without running away in the many ways in which this is customarily done.

The beginning of the practice of concentration will be difficult; it will appear as if one could never achieve the aim. That this implies the necessity to have patience need hardly be said. If one does not know that everything has its time, and wants to force things, then indeed one will never succeed in becoming concentrated—nor in the art of loving. To have an idea of what patience is one need only watch a child learning to walk. It falls, falls again, and falls again, and yet it goes on trying, improving, until one day it walks without falling. What could the grown-up person achieve if he had the child's patience and its concentration in the pursuits which are important to him!   ERICH FROMM

A Happy Man

To awaken each morning with a smile brightening my face; to greet the day with reverence for the opportunities it contains; to approach my work with cheerfulness and pleasure; to hold ever before me, even in the doing of little things, the Purpose toward which I am working; to meet men and women with laughter on my lips and love in my heart; to be gentle, kind, and courteous through all the hours; to approach the night with weariness that ever woos sleep and the joy that comes from work well done—this is how I desire to live wisely my days.

THOMAS DEKKER

Today and Tomorrow

Happy the man, and happy he alone,
    He who can call today his own.
He who, secure within, can say,
    Tomorrow, do thy worst, for I have lived today!

JOHN DRYDEN

The world
Is after all as the butterfly,
However it may be.
SOIN

Slow days passing, accumulating,
How distant they are,
The things of the past!
BUSON

My eyes, having seen all,
Came back to
　　The white chrysanthemums.
　　　　　ISSHO

Just simply alive,
Both of us, I
　　And the poppy.
　　　　　ISSA

How admirable,
He who thinks not, "Life is fleeting,"
　　When he sees the lightning!
　　　　　BASHO

The short night;
The peony opened
　　During that time.
　　　　　BUSON

The first dream of the year;
I kept it a secret
　　And smiled to myself.
　　　　　SHO-U

How many, many things
They call to mind,
   These cherry-blossoms!
       BASHO

The night-light goes out;
The sound of the water:
   The coolness.
       SHIKI

Calm days,
The swift years
   Forgotten.
       TAIGI

Yield to the willow
All the loathing, all the desire
   Of your heart.
       BASHO

Tranquility:
Walking alone;
   Happy alone.
       SHIKI

It arose a perfect sphere—
But how long it is,
   This spring day!
      TERITOKU

In a short life,
An hour of leisure,
   This autumn evening.
      BUSON

Composed in Intertype Garamond,
a classic version of Claude Garamond's design;
first specimens are found in books
printed in Paris circa 1532.
Printed on Hallmark Eggshell Book Paper.
Designed by John Hackler